YOGA COLORING BOOK

From The Sphinx to Taj Mahal

ARTHUR BENJAMIN

This page intentionally left blank.

ABOUT THE BOOK

Explore the sensual beauty of these unique landscapes together with perfect harmony and balance of these yoga poses. Including 8 gorgeous coloring illustrations, these will take you to 8 enchanted places from Egypt to Rio de Janeiro to the Taj Mahal.

Printed in the United States of America
ISBN: 978-1619495340

CONTENTS

This page intentionally left blank.

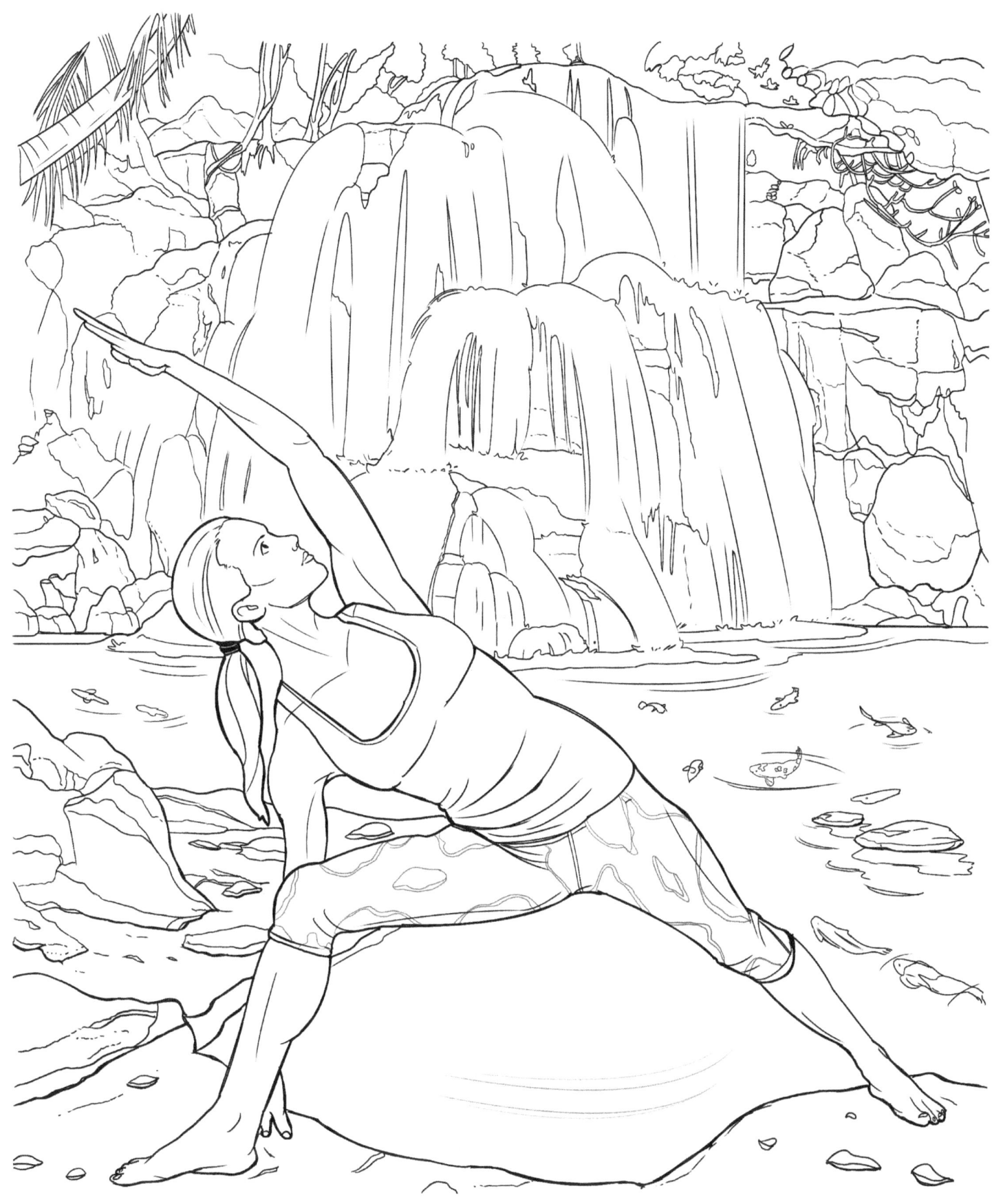

Plate 1.
Extended Side Angle Pose

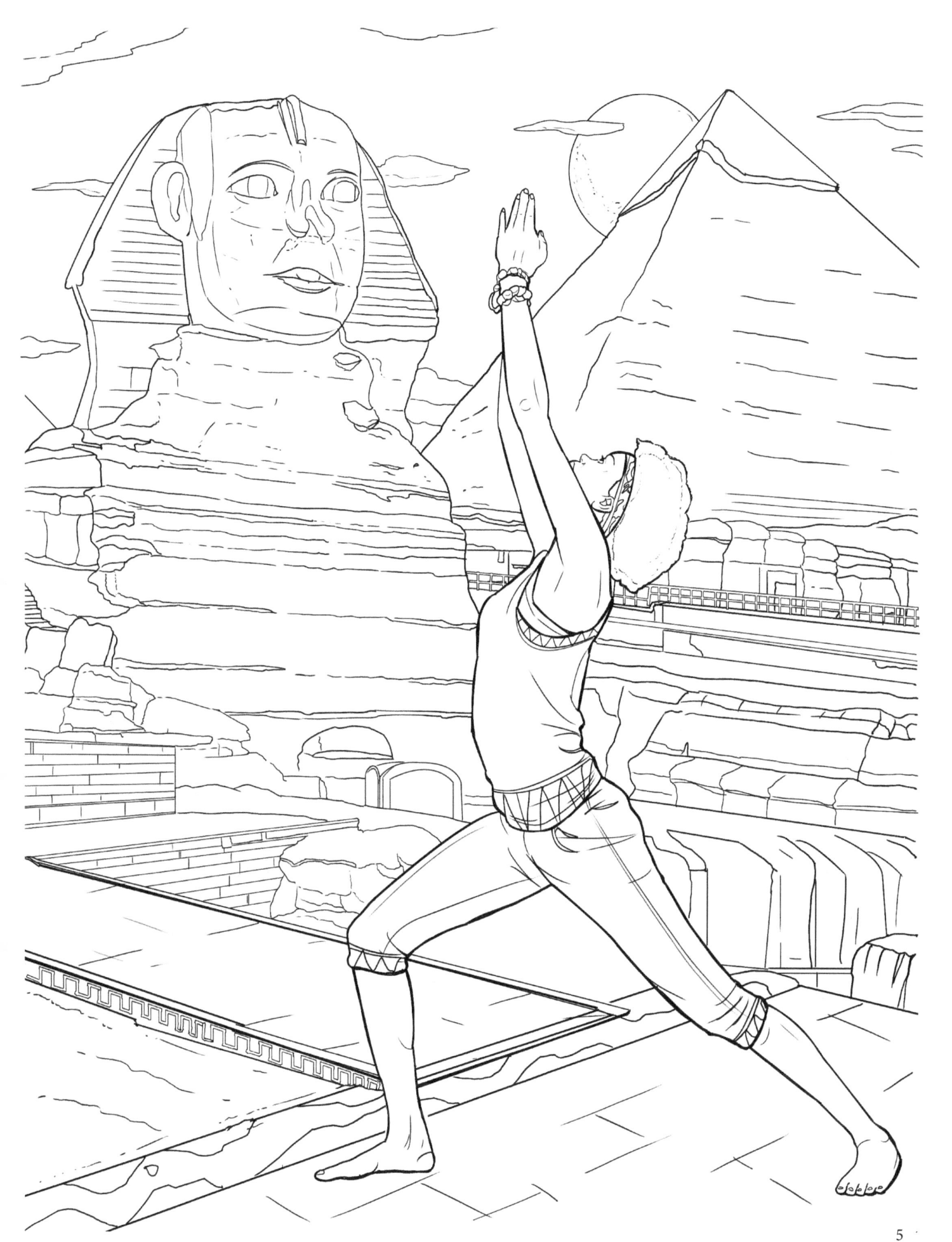

Plate 2.
Warrior Pose

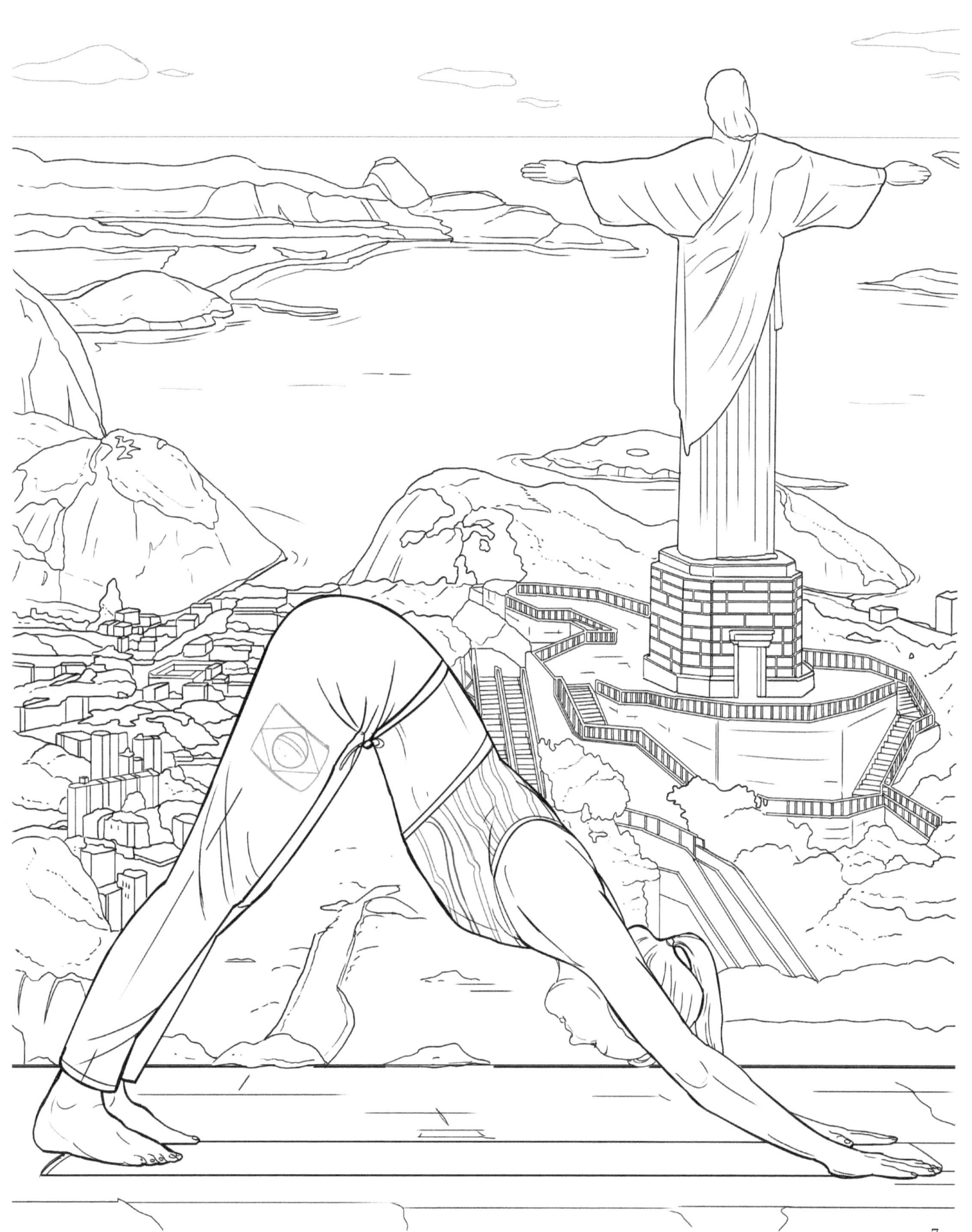

Plate 3.
Downward Facing Dog

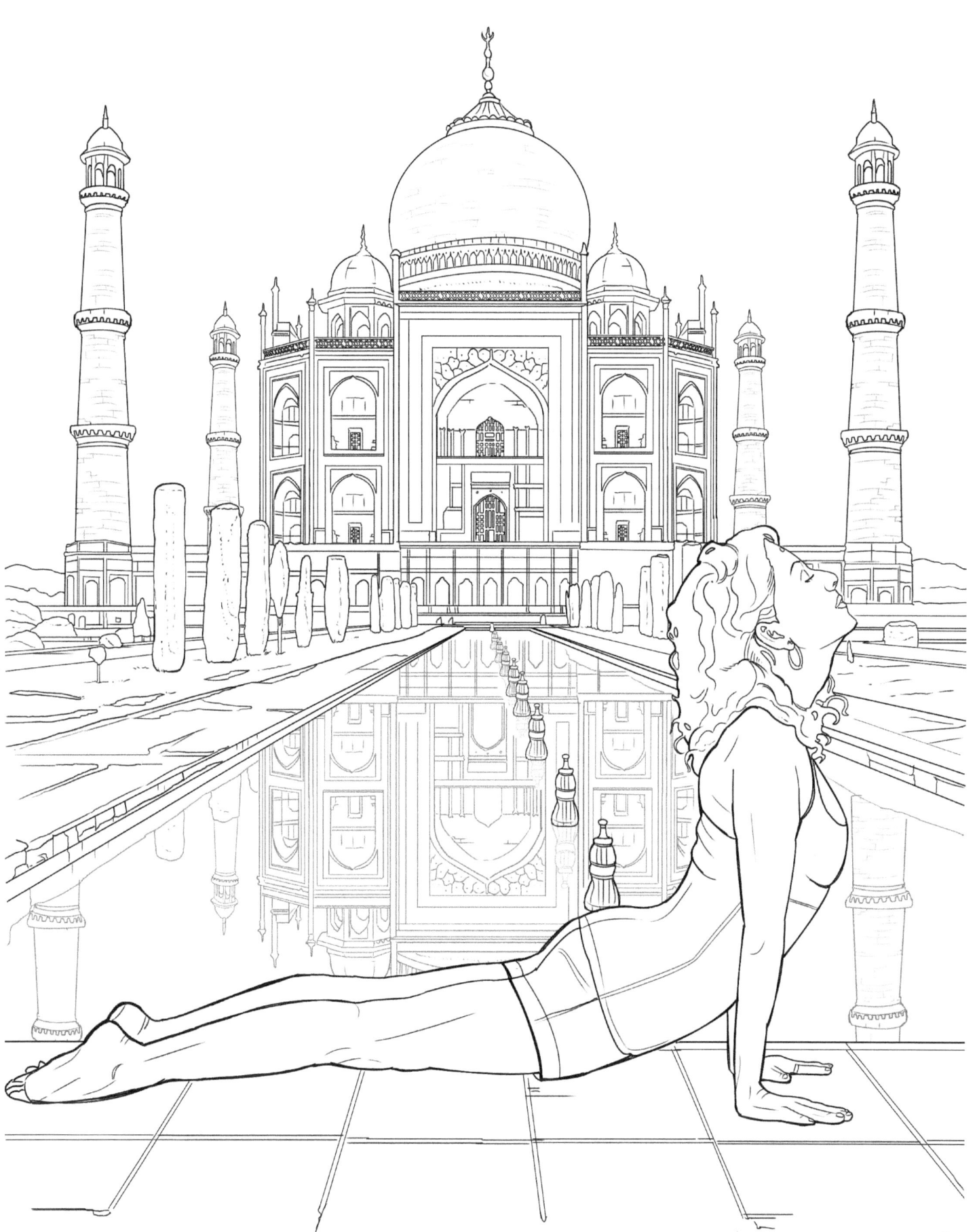

Plate 4.
Upward Facing Dog

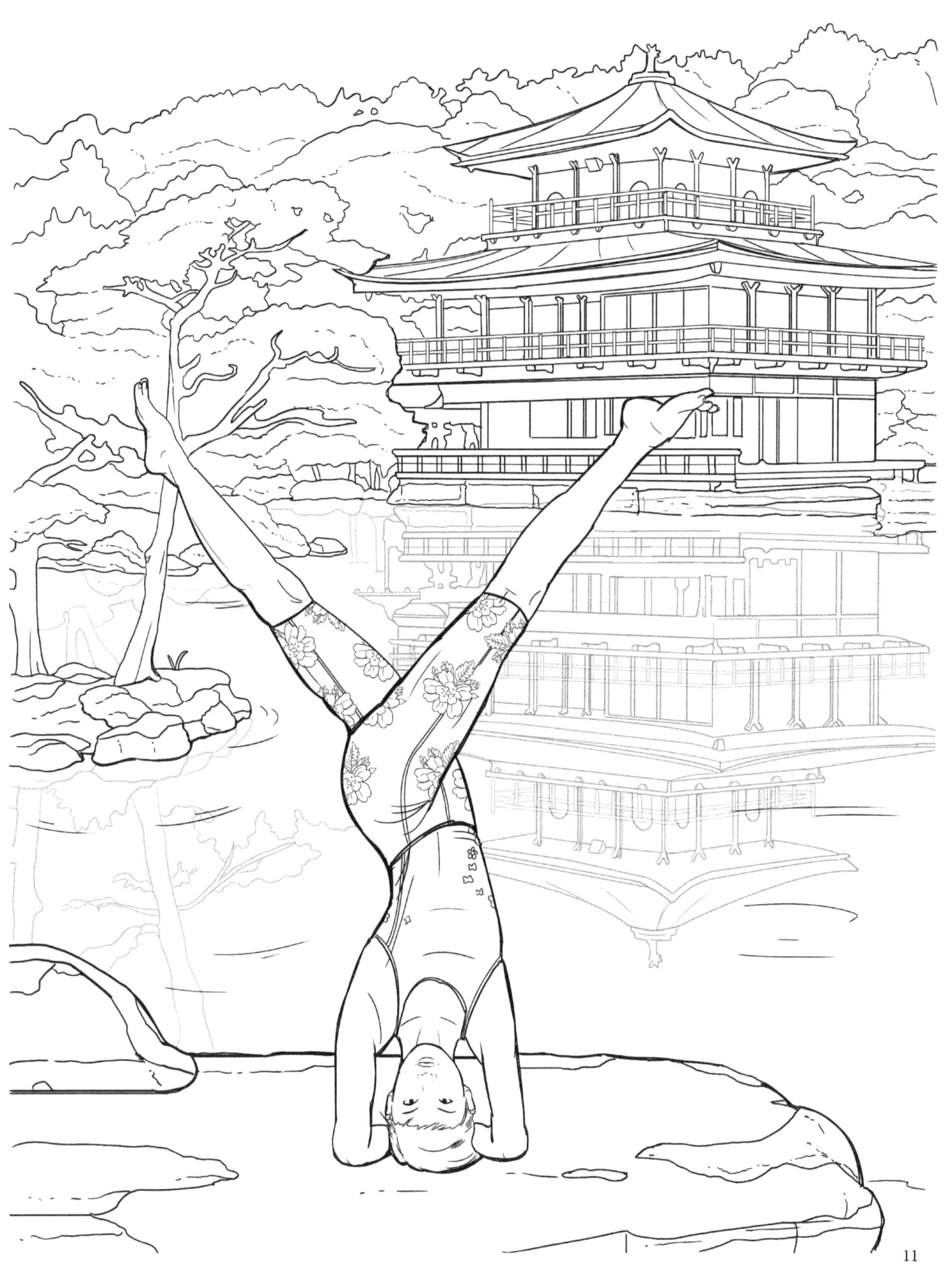

Plate 5.

Revolved Headstand

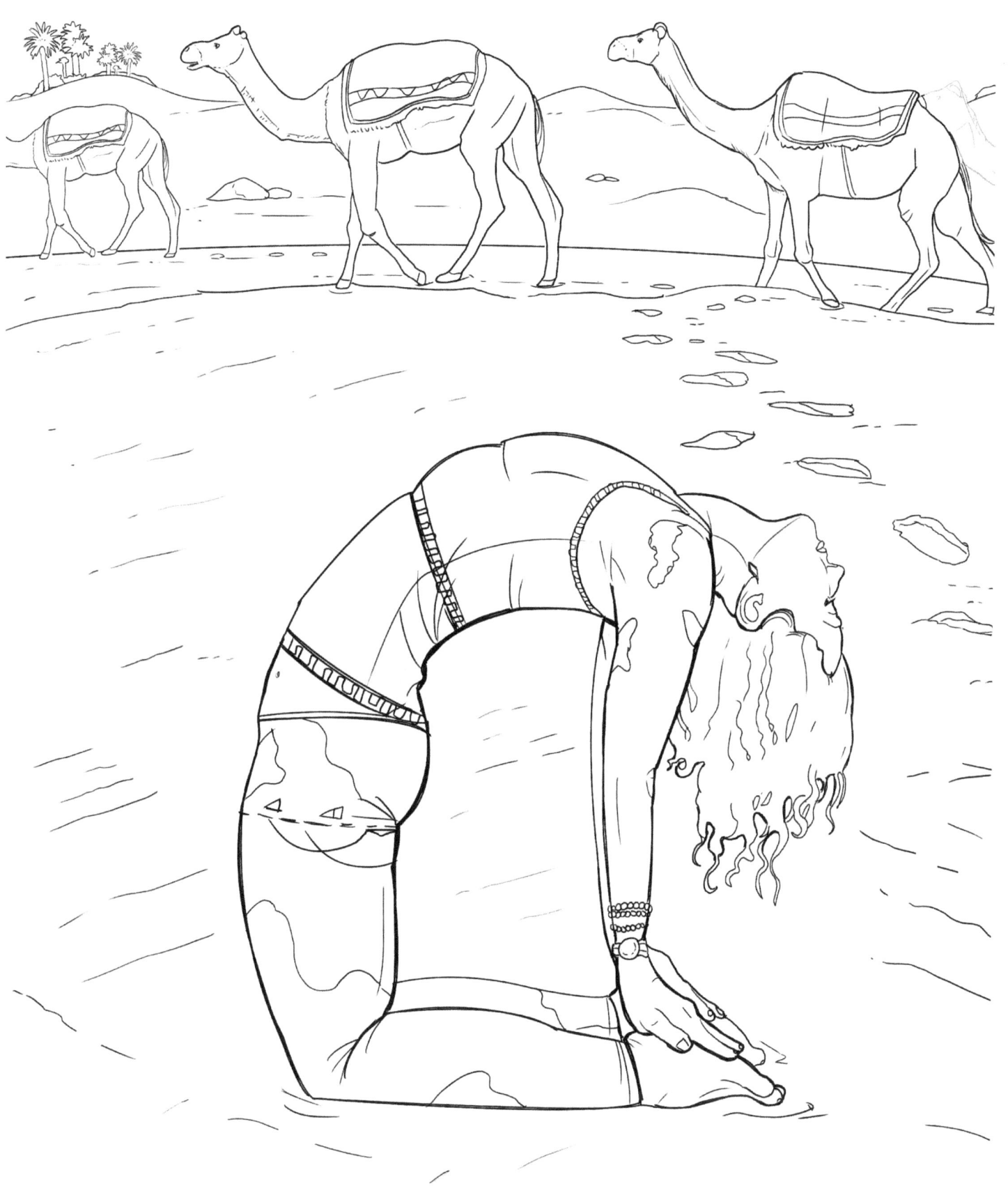

Plate 6.
Camel Pose

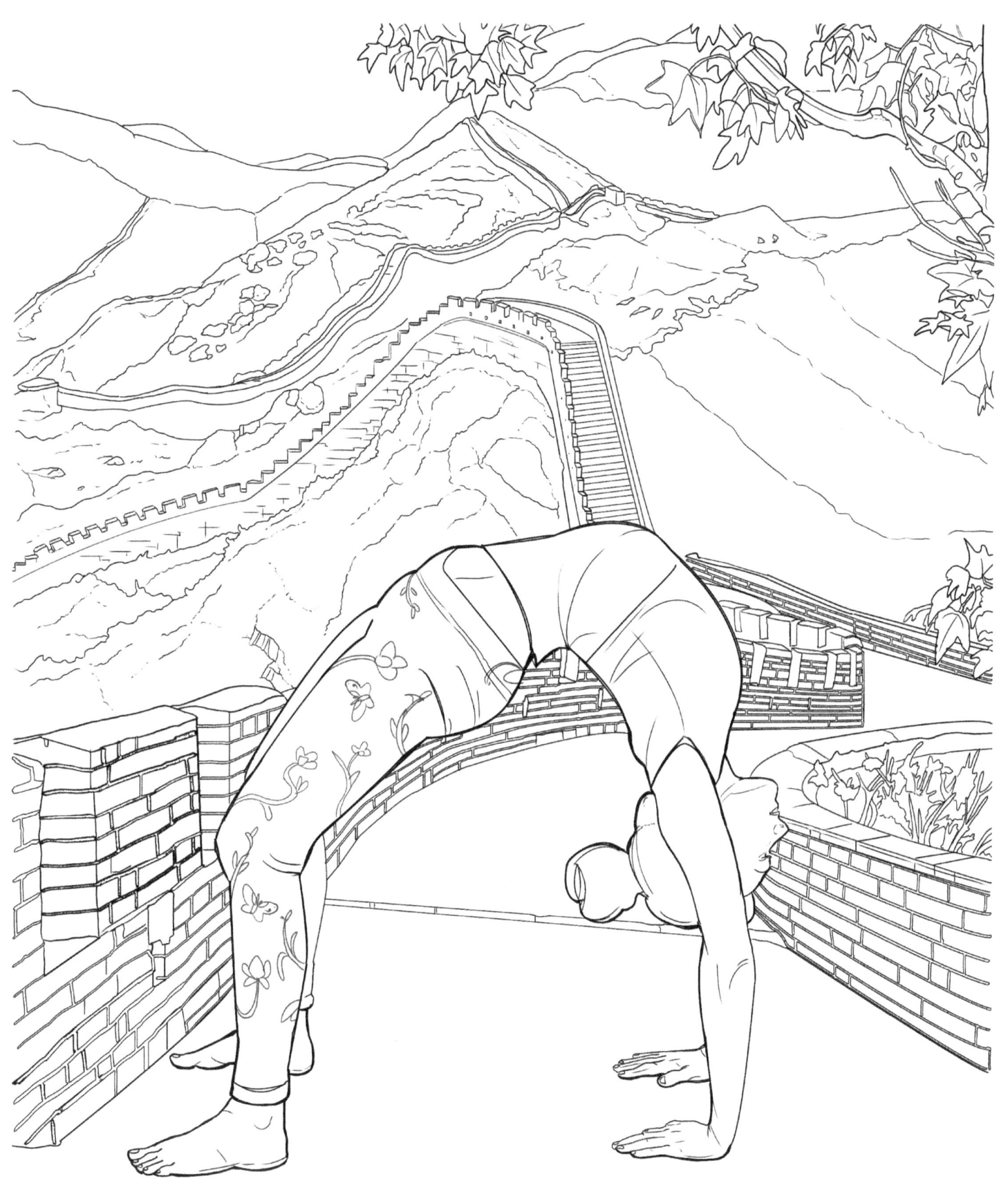

Plate 7.
Upward Facing Bow Pose

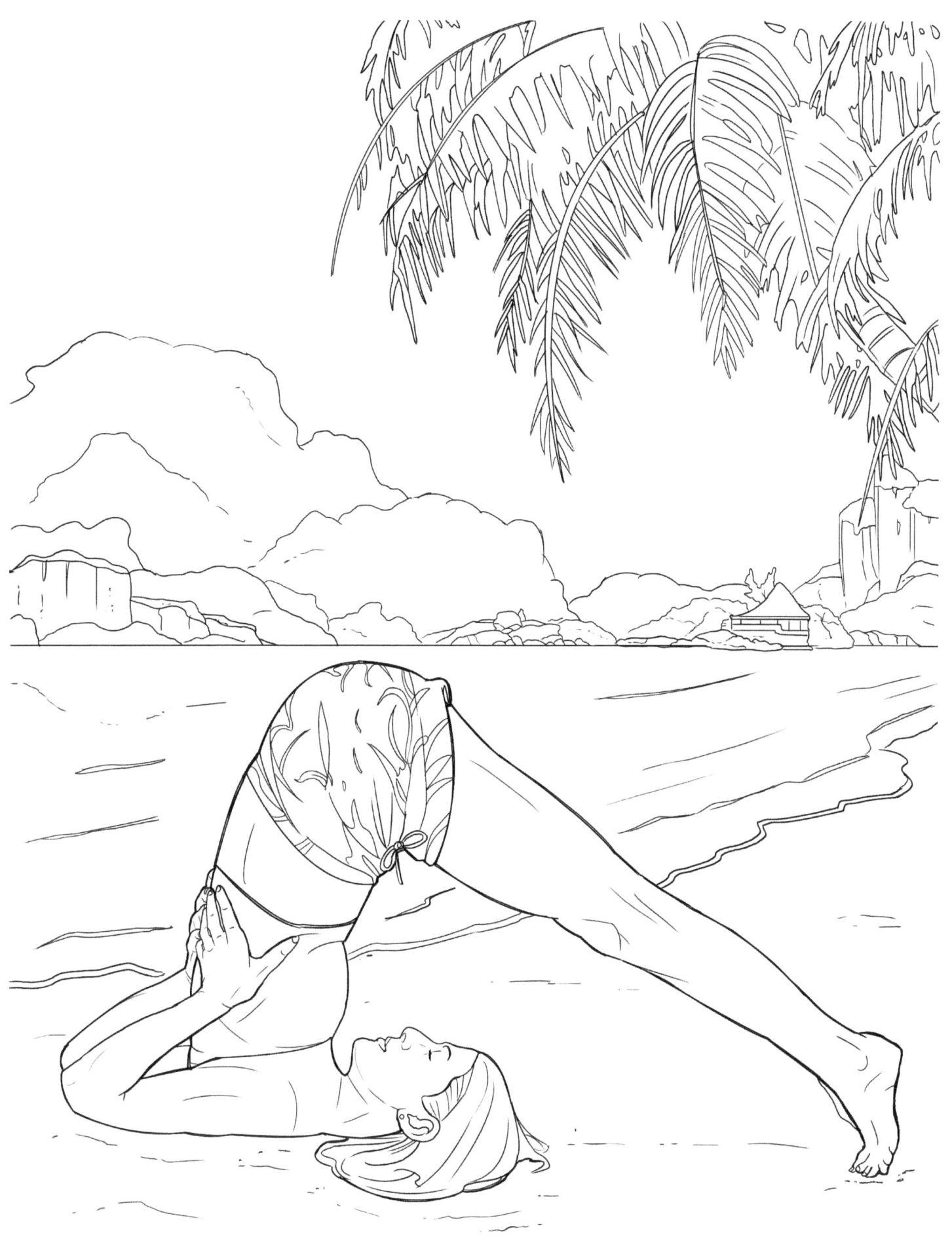

Plate 8.
Plow Pose

ABOUT THE BOOK

Explore the sensual beauty of these unique landscapes together with perfect harmony and balance of these yoga poses. Including 8 gorgeous coloring illustrations, these will take you to 8 enchanted places from Egypt to Rio de Janeiro to the Taj Mahal.

This page intentionally left blank.

www.ingramcontent.com/pod-product-compliance
Lightning Source LLC
Chambersburg PA
CBHW081307170526
45165CB00010B/3290